Lent and Holy Week with Saint Joseph

Lent and Holy Week with
Saint Joseph

Reflections by the Affiliates
of Mayslake Ministries

Edited by Dr. Mary Amore

Our Sunday Visitor
Huntington, Indiana

27 26 25 24 23 22 1 2 3 4 5 6 7 8 9

Our Sunday Visitor Publishing Division
Our Sunday Visitor, Inc.
200 Noll Plaza
Huntington, IN 46750
www.osv.com
1-800-348-2440

ISBN: 978-1-63966-014-8 (Inventory No. T2752)
1 RELIGION—Holidays—Easter & Lent.
2 RELIGION—Christianity—Saints & Sainthood.
3 RELIGION—Christianity—Catholic.

LCCN: 2022942042

Cover and interior design: Lindsey Riesen
Cover art: Adobe Stock

Printed in the United States of America

~ Reflections ~

Ash Wednesday: Faithfulness

Now faith is the assurance of things hoped for, the conviction of things not seen. — Hebrews 11:1

As a Boy Scout, I participated in a team building activity called trust walks. A blindfolded boy received guidance from his partner to walk around obstacles using verbal or nonverbal instructions. There were times when blindfolded that I did not trust my partner, and as a result, both of us fell to the ground. When it was my turn to lead my blindfolded partner, there were moments of hesitation, doubt, or uncertainty which caused us to stumble and fall.

Saint Joseph's faith journey can be characterized as a trust walk. Saint Joseph placed his complete faith in the Lord, not knowing what tomorrow would bring, and followed God. In times of hesitation or self-doubt, let us turn to Saint Joseph for guidance so that we may place our trust in the workings of the Lord as he did.

– Deacon Jerry Souta

REFLECT ON YOUR "trust walk" with the Lord. Are you open to allowing the Lord to lead and guide you, especially when you are "blindfolded"? Seek the help of Saint Joseph to strengthen your faith and trust in God.

Prayer: Saint Joseph, you demonstrated great faith even in the most challenging of circumstances. Increase my trust in the Lord that I may follow in your footsteps as I walk my journey of faith. Amen.

Thursday after Ash Wednesday: Obedience

But he said, "Blessed rather are those who hear the word of God and keep it!" — Luke 11:28

To practice obedience, we must learn the art of listening. Sacred listening formed Joseph's heart. Joseph and Mary are called holy because they heard the word of God, received it into their hearts, and then responded.

Joseph responded to God with actions. His fiat was first given when the angel came to him in a dream. Joseph awoke and did as the angel instructed.

God also spoke through the law and the prophets. Joseph was a faithful Jew, and he obediently carried out the precepts of the law prescribed in his duties as a loving husband and father. The circumcision, the presentation in the Temple, the naming of Jesus: These were all the duties of the Jewish father.

In order to obey God's word, we must learn to be quiet and listen, then consider how we might act. By listening in prayer, we can learn to express our own fiat — that is, "let it be done." Saint Joseph is here to help us.

— Sr. Mary McNulty

Is there space in your life to listen and respond?

Prayer: Saint Joseph, you awoke and did as the angel instructed. Instruct my heart to hear God's word and respond to God's will in my life. Amen.

Friday after Ash Wednesday: Courage

God is our refuge and strength,
a very present help in trouble.
— Psalm 46:1

As a man of God, Joseph stayed out of trouble. He followed the laws of his time and was a good neighbor and friend. In order to comply with Caesar's census, Joseph had to return to his birthplace, Bethlehem, with Mary to be counted. He had the courage to do what was expected, even though Mary was about to give birth, and they made the trip. The journey that Mary and Joseph took was arduous, yet Joseph prevailed: He courageously protected Mary and her newborn Son.

Joseph's courage came from his deep faith in God, in whom he found refuge and strength. Joseph obeyed civil authorities that imposed rules and regulations that were at times unjust. But Joseph had the courage to follow the laws of the land and the Law of the Lord. Saint Joseph can help us be good citizens of the world and good citizens of God's kingdom.

— Alice Smith

Consider the ways that Saint Joseph's life can help you to courageously follow God in the midst of a culture of sin and death.

Prayer: Saint Joseph, provide the courage I need to assess my duties as a good citizen and a faithful follower of Christ. Amen.

Saturday after Ash Wednesday: Self-Control

For God did not give us a spirit of timidity but a spirit of power and love and self-control. — 2 Timothy 1:7

What is self-control? A hefty dose of sheer willpower? A personality trait? A result of training? Scripture tells us that it is God's gift, not one we receive passively, but actively. Receiving the grace of self-control means allowing God to work in our hearts. Self-control helps us to resist temptation and avoid conforming to the things of this world. It guides our decisions and behavior.

There must have been times when Joseph became frustrated with young Jesus as he learned the skills of carpentry. I imagine that like any parent, Joseph had to practice self-control so he would not become irritated or impatient. In those parental moments, Joseph surely allowed God to work in his heart.

— Kristy DeSanti

In what area of your life do you desire to resist temptation? Who do you want to show love and patience to today? Seek the help of Saint Joseph to give you a spirit of self-control.

Prayer: Saint Joseph, please help me to ask for and receive the gift of self-control. May it create changes in my heart so that I can resist temptation and reflect more of God's love to the world. Amen.

~ Faithfulness ~

First Week of Lent, Sunday

Where you go I will go, and where you lodge I will lodge; your people shall be my people, and your God my God.
— Ruth 1:16

Scripture tells us that, at first, Joseph struggled with the news of Mary's pregnancy and he was going to divorce her quietly to protect her. Yet after the angel told him not to be afraid, he took Mary into his home.

Joseph's faithfulness to Mary reminds me of my own marriage. My husband's name is Joseph (Mary and Joseph!), and during forty-five years, we have remained faithful to each other, a faithfulness rooted in our love for God and our commitment to each other.

Joseph was steadfast in his commitment to love and care for Mary and Jesus. Wherever their journey took them, Joseph provided food and lodging and kept them safe from all harm. The life of Joseph as husband and father shows us how important faithfulness is in our relationships.

— Dr. Mary Amore

Do you struggle with being faithful in your relationships? Seek the help of Saint Joseph that you may be faithful and loyal in your dealings with others.

Prayer: Saint Joseph, husband of Mary and father of Jesus, help me to deepen my faithfulness to God and to those in my family. Amen.

First Week of Lent, Monday

His master said to him, "Well done, good and faithful servant; you have been faithful over a little, I will set you over much." — Matthew 25:21

In Scripture, we hear that Joseph was a righteous man, and in the short time that we encounter him, we see clearly that he was. Joseph did all that God asked of him — whether he was told not to divorce Mary, or to travel to Egypt and back with his family, he promptly took action.

Not only was Joseph faithful to God, but he was also faithful to the promises he made to Mary and Jesus. He actively supported and protected them. Joseph's faithfulness is why God chose him to be Jesus' earthly father. Joseph had proven his fidelity; therefore, God made him the guardian of Our Lord and Savior. He was given the awesome responsibility of not only protecting Jesus but teaching and guiding him in his early life. Joseph was faithful both in his love for God and in his love for those entrusted to his care.

— Maria Pusateri

WHAT ABOUT US? Are we faithful to the responsibilities we have been given? When called upon, do we promptly do what God asks?

Prayer: Saint Joseph, help me to be faithful so that one day I may hear, "Well done my good and faithful servant." Amen.

First Week of Lent, Tuesday

No temptation has overtaken you that is not common to man. God is faithful, and he will not let you be tempted beyond your strength, but with the temptation will also provide the way of escape, that you may be able to endure it. — 1 Corinthians 10:13

When trials come into my life, when I am overwhelmed, faith reminds me that God is truly faithful, that he is with me, lighting the path I am to take. When I follow his lead, I have nothing to fear.

I often look to Saint Joseph for inspiration in parenting. Joseph was a faith-filled man who experienced the trials of life in ways we could never imagine. Yet he remained faithful to the Lord and depended on his faith to help him to follow God's plan for his family. A good and faithful husband and father, Joseph was able to embrace the goodness of the Lord, even in the midst of difficulties. His life has much to teach us.

— Gina Sannasardo

Are there times in your life when you are wavering in your faith? Turn to Saint Joseph to help you deepen your faith in God so that you can overcome all difficulties.

Prayer: Saint Joseph, father of my Savior, when I am weak, strengthen me in faith that I may cast aside all fear and doubt and follow the ways of the Lord. Amen.

First Week of Lent, Wednesday

The steadfast love of the Lord never ceases,
his mercies never come to an end;
they are new every morning;
great is your faithfulness.
— Lamentations 3:22–23

There's a window I love to sit by to view the sunrise through the trees and across the landscape and housetops. The spectacle is a transcendent reminder of God's faithfulness. The sun is rising everywhere in the world, "new every morning," as Scripture says.

I often forget to take in the faithfulness of God's gifts of nature and abundance. I get too busy, which hampers me from returning faithfulness to God by spending time in prayer and service, by living in a way that reflects the depth of God's faithfulness to me. Caring for Mary and parenting Jesus, Saint Joseph reminds me how to receive and return God's faithfulness. He responded faithfully to God's call and was open to the Holy Spirit guiding his daily life.

— Dr. Barbara Jarvis-Pauls

Consider your own life. Is there a way to establish time in your daily schedule to reflect on and appreciate God's abiding faithfulness? Like Saint Joseph, how have you answered God's call in your life?

Prayer: Saint Joseph, pray for me to be more aware of the faithfulness of God's love and beauty of creation in my life. Amen.

First Week of Lent, Thursday

You shall be careful to do therefore as the Lord your God has commanded you; you shall not turn aside to the right hand or to the left. You shall walk in all the way which the Lord your God has commanded you, that you may live, and that it may go well with you. — Deuteronomy 5:32–33

Saint Joseph's voice is silent in the Gospel. None of his words are recorded. Yet he is certainly one of our greatest role models. His silence cannot be understood as apathy because his actions were so bold.

Saint Joseph showed his faithfulness by allowing God to lead the way. He was a man who, regardless of any inner struggles, faithfully followed the promptings of the Spirit. Like Joseph, we all face trials. Sometimes our own plans and expectations must change dramatically. Often, we do not know what to do or where to turn. Saint Joseph teaches us to trust God completely and with every detail of our lives.

— Lori Bertucci-Thibeau

Take time with Saint Joseph and ask him to share with you how he was able to remain faithful and persevere even when exhausted. As you clear your mind and relax, listen for his encouragement and his love.

Prayer: Saint Joseph, help me to listen and surrender. Show me how to become quiet and peaceful so I may better see God's will and follow it. Amen.

First Week of Lent, Friday

And her husband Joseph, being a just man and unwilling to put her to shame, resolved to send her away quietly.
— Matthew 1:19

Faithfulness is the quality of being steadfast, reliant, faithful, unfailing, and remaining loyal no matter circumstances or costs. It is not duty; it is not exhibition. It is defining one's life in the context of others.

According to the laws and customs of their day, Joseph and Mary's betrothal meant they were already considered husband and wife, with all the full legal rights that marriage would seal. The contractual agreements had been reached, and the consents had been given. So you can imagine the crisis that Mary's announcement brought. The law gave Joseph rights and authority, but Joseph chose faithfulness instead, staying true to his word, no matter the circumstance or the cost to himself.

Faithfulness is just one of God's unchanging attributes. God always does what he promises, always keeps his word to us. And it is this promise of faithfulness that is the foundation of our hope.

— Colleen Case

WHERE HAVE YOU SEEN God's faithfulness in your life? Where do you need God's faithfulness?

Prayer: Blessed Saint Joseph, pray for me, that I may come to know the faithfulness of God, our Father. Amen.

First Week of Lent, Saturday

Your faithfulness endures to all generations;
you have established the earth, and it stands fast.
— Psalm 119:90

As a devout Jew, Joseph would have been familiar with all the stories of another Joseph, the son of Jacob. He would have known him being sold into slavery by his brothers, falsely accused, and imprisoned. He would have also heard of Joseph's faithfulness to God's will through it all. How even though his brothers had betrayed him, Joseph was faithful and saved their lives from famine. He would learn to see the faithfulness of God in every circumstance and trust that God was at work in every instant to bring about good.

Saint Joseph's life was full of uncertainty as well. Yet he, too, was faithful through it all. He was faithful in fulfilling God's will by protecting Mary and her unborn Son, by traveling to Bethlehem where Jesus was to be born, and by fleeing to Egypt, the land where Joseph of old had been blessed.

— Denine Chambers

Is there a situation in your life where you struggle to see God at work? Let these stories be a reminder of God's faithfulness in all situations. And let us be like these great men in our faithfulness to God.

Prayer: Saint Joseph, help me to remain faithful in doing God's will. Amen.

~ Obedience ~

Second Week of Lent, Sunday

And the Lord came and stood forth, calling as at other times, "Samuel! Samuel!" And Samuel said, "Speak, for your servant hears." — 1 Samuel 3:10

How often do we hear a quiet voice and ignore it? Or have a feeling that we should be doing something, or praying for someone, and brush it off as nonsense? A friend of mine was praying one day and felt he needed to pray for my daughter. When he told me this later, I was shocked because she had been having a tough time and needed prayer at that moment. My friend was obedient to the inspiration he had received.

Like Samuel, Joseph heard the call of God several times and obeyed. Sacred Scripture writes of those big moments in Joseph's life when he was obedient, but it is likely that Joseph was also obedient to God in small ways we will never know of. Perhaps God nudged Joseph during his busy days at work to pray for Jesus or Mary. In matters big and small, Joseph was obedient to the call of God.

— Lauren Nelson

Spend time today listening. Who is God inviting you to pray for?

Prayer: Saint Joseph, help me to have a servant's heart, filled with love and obedience, that I may serve the Lord in the people that God places in my life. Amen.

Second Week of Lent, Monday

But be doers of the word, and not hearers only, deceiving yourselves. — James 1:22

The secular world tells us that our true freedom lies in taking control of our own lives — but is this really the correct way of thinking? Submitting to authority is not easy, for it demands trust to do so. Joseph trusted God completely, and this allowed him to say "yes" to God's invitation. He gave his fiat just as Mary did. God did not force him to do this; Joseph did this of his own free will.

Joseph had his own dreams for his life with Mary; God had other ideas. He desired Joseph to participate in his plan as the earthly father of his Son, Jesus. Joseph's profound faith in God enabled him to listen to God's word and respond in obedience. His life is an inspiration for all of us. In order to participate in God's plan, we must allow God to be in control. When we align our will to God's will, we become truly free.

— Maria Pusateri

ARE YOU READY TO give up control, put your trust in God, and live in his freedom?

Prayer: Saint Joseph, help me to hear God's word and freely choose to obey it. Amen.

Second Week of Lent, Tuesday

Now therefore, if you will obey my voice and keep my covenant, you shall be my own possession among all peoples.
— Exodus 19:5

Saint Joseph offers us an example of how to live obediently and to love the Lord faithfully, even when life is complicated. When Joseph initially heard of Mary's pregnancy, he struggled and he prayed to God that he would do the right and just thing for Mary in this precarious situation.

There are times when I find myself asking, "What is the right thing to do?" More often than not, there is no easy answer, nor is the solution clearly marked out on my journey of faith. We can turn to Saint Joseph for help to lead and guide us when we are unclear of the path ahead. He is our spiritual father, and he is here to help us obey the voice of our God.

— Deacon Jerry Souta

Recall a time when you were unsure of what the "right thing" was. Where did you turn for an answer? Today, invite Saint Joseph into your life to lead and guide your steps that you may faithfully follow the ways of the Lord.

Prayer: Saint Joseph, teach me how to obey so that my life may bear great fruit for the kingdom of God. Amen.

Second Week of Lent, Wednesday

When Joseph woke from sleep, he did as the angel of the Lord commanded him; he took his wife. — Matthew 1:24

While I have always known of Saint Joseph's obedience to God, it was not until I became a parent that I marveled at his quiet and humble obedience. Never do we read in the New Testament that Saint Joseph stood up and proclaimed, "Look at me! Aren't I amazing? Without me, none of this would have happened!"

As much as I chuckle at the thought, I recall a few times when I craved some recognition for the sacrifices I had made for my family. Joseph did not. Instead, he displayed quiet obedience by trusting God at great expense. He did not dwell on whether he would be recognized or respected by others. He did not announce his sacrifices from the mountain tops, or tell others hoping that his actions would earn him a reputation for holiness. It was enough for him to carry out the will of God in quiet obedience. Whatever it is that makes us yearn for attention can decrease if we follow Saint Joseph's example.

— Meg Bucaro

WHAT OR WHO ARE you struggling to obey today? Seek the help of Saint Joseph in your endeavor.

Prayer: Saint Joseph, please help me to obey God's will for me today, without attention or recognition. Amen.

Second Week of Lent, Thursday

As he said this, a woman in the crowd raised her voice and said to him, "Blessed is the womb that bore you, and the breasts that you sucked!" But he said, "Blessed rather are those who hear the word of God and keep it!" — Luke 11:27–28

Jesus does not rebuke the woman's remarks concerning Mary's role as his mother. Instead, he emphasizes her obedience to his word: this — and not her biological role — is how Mary attains her greatness. As the spouse of Mary, Saint Joseph also was obedient to the Lord. He submitted to God and showed his love by doing what was asked of him, even in the most extraordinary of circumstances.

Joseph's life of obedience to God invites us to follow him. We acknowledge the Lord's authority by hearing, trusting, and surrendering to his word. The Lord blesses us when we put into practice in our daily lives the word of God. Through obedience, we demonstrate our love of God, and we become transformed as we grow spiritually. We do not live a fully developed obedient life overnight, but we grow in holiness as we grow in obedience.

— Donna Soukup

What is your lifelong plan for observing God's word?

Prayer: Saint Joseph, pray for me to grow in obedience to God's word. Amen.

Second Week of Lent, Friday

And he rose and took the child and his mother, and went to the land of Israel. — Matthew 2:21

Obedience is not merely an action, it is a decision, an act of trust placed in something greater than ourselves. It is a willingness to have one's affections and conduct aligned with God. Joseph's life was a journey of obedience. Again and again, Joseph's actions demonstrated a desire to do God's will. Joseph knew that doing what God asked was both a choice and a response of love. Imagine how different the story of salvation history would be had Joseph not obeyed God.

Obedience to God opens to us a space that nothing else can. When we enact our will in alignment with God's will, as Saint Joseph did, we are entering love itself. Love and obedience are inextricably connected. One is the expression of the other.

— Colleen Case

WHAT COMES TO MIND when you hear the word *obedience*? Does it stir a desire to comply or resist? Think of a time you did obey God. What were the blessings that you received as a result?

Prayer: Blessed Saint Joseph, help me learn the joy and gift of obedience. Pray for me that I may know that God is trustworthy and may lovingly respond to God's love. Help me to follow your example of obedience. Amen.

Second Week of Lent, Saturday

My son, keep your father's commandment,
and forsake not your mother's teaching.
Bind them upon your heart always;
tie them about your neck.
— Proverbs 6:20–21

It is much easier to be obedient when we understand the "why" and the "what." When obedience is on our terms, we feel some sense of control rather than just blindly diving in. We live in a space between what the world asks of us and what God invites us to do. Fear of the unknown is a thread that runs through all of humanity, and trust is a word that few understand anymore. Yet, God asks us not only to trust him but also to obey, often without knowing the "why."

Saint Joseph can help us to follow the way of the Lord. As the spouse of Mary, Joseph trusted completely in God, and obeyed the will of the Lord even when the circumstances of his situation did not make sense. Let us follow in his steps.

— Lori Bertucci-Thibeau

How do we resolve the inner conflict we experience between obedience and fear or uncertainty? Where do we turn?

Prayer: Saint Joseph, help me to strive for a deeper faith in God, that I may be totally obedient to God even when I don't understand the "what" or "why" of his will. Amen.

~ Love ~

Third Week of Lent, Sunday

Where did this man get this wisdom and these mighty works? Is not this the carpenter's son? — Matthew 13:54–55

In his public ministry, Jesus offered miraculous healings and revealed parables to eager crowds. Some, however, were perplexed. To them, Jesus was just "the carpenter's son," so they struggled to understand how he could become capable of these mighty works.

As a boy, Jesus would have accompanied Joseph in the workshop and on the job site. He would have observed the devotion and attention to detail needed to create a craftsman's masterpiece imbued with quality and beauty. He learned the importance of love, respect, and patience with whatever materials needed transformation — whether wood, metal, or human souls.

Joseph loved Jesus and was fully aware of the responsibility that God had entrusted to him by placing Jesus in his care. He built and shaped the Holy Family as a carpenter would, with the same artistry and love he used every day in his work. The fruit of Joseph's love can be seen in the wisdom and works of Jesus.

— Curt Paddock

ARE THERE WAYS TO express in your relationships the kind of love and care a craftsman expresses in his work?

Prayer: Saint Joseph, help me to grow in the art of loving those entrusted to me. Amen.

Third Week of Lent, Monday

With all lowliness and meekness, with patience, forbearing one another in love. — Ephesians 4:2

Joseph had a deep love for God, and this love allowed him to pour himself out freely and willingly in service to the Lord. It was love that moved Saint Joseph to make his marriage, family, and work an offering of humble service to the Lord.

Today's culture bombards us with various images of romantic love. While no one disputes the thrill of feeling butterflies, we all know that genuine love goes deeper than that. Love is not about feelings. It is, as St. Thomas Aquinas says, "willing the good of another," even when that requires self-sacrifice.

Joseph also loved unconditionally. Unconditional love reflects back the love we have received from God, our Creator, and find its culmination in service. That is the love Saint Joseph freely gave to Mary and Jesus. It is the love that bears fruit and stands the test of time.

— Lori Bertucci-Thibeau

TAKE SOME TIME TODAY in the loving embrace of Saint Joseph. Let his silent way of love fill you and give you strength.

Prayer: Saint Joseph, I know our loving God demands something of me. Help me to model my life after yours, as a gift of loving service. Amen.

Third Week of Lent, Tuesday

Truly, I say to you, this poor widow has put in more than all those who are contributing to the treasury. For they all contributed out of their abundance; but she out of her poverty has put in everything she had, her whole living. — Mark 12:43–44

Sometimes it's much easier to avoid someone or turn away than it is to love them. There are a hundred excuses not to extend myself, not to give, not to be loving. When I sit in solitude before the Lord, however, I am reminded of what love requires. I realize that sometimes my desire to be right is an obstacle to love. I recall that love speaks louder in action than it does in words and that more blessings come from giving than from receiving.

Through prayer, I come to understand that the life of Joseph was one of quiet, loving action as he stood by Mary, supporting, protecting, and guiding her — not with what he had left over, but with his all. Are we not called to follow the example of Saint Joseph in our own lives?

— Marianne Patrovito

WHO CAN YOU lovingly serve this day? Are you giving out of your "leftovers," or offering all you have in love?

Prayer: Saint Joseph, may I follow your example of selfless love in action. Amen.

Third Week of Lent, Wednesday

I am my beloved's and my beloved is mine. — Song of Solomon 6:3

From the moment Joseph took Mary into his home, he was steadfast in his love for Mary and Our Lord. Together they built a life centered on their love for God and each other. Though their days were filled with prayer, work, service, laughter, and tears, Joseph and Mary remained each other's biggest support and constant beloved. They upheld each other in every circumstance, praising God for all their blessings. Their mutual love for God and one another provided the foundation for Jesus to grow into his mission.

As a Catholic couple, my husband and I prioritize each other. We both hold our mutual love for God above our relationships. Christian marriage comes with the important responsibility of helping your spouse get to heaven. Love of God and love of spouse are the heart of a Christian marriage. We belong to each other because we belong to God. We love because we are also beloved.

— Amy Bovie

As the beloved, how do you show your love for God and others daily?

Prayer: Saint Joseph, please help heal broken marriages and restore the sanctity of marriage and family to the elevation of God's design. Amen.

Third Week of Lent, Thursday

God is love, and he who abides in love abides in God, and God abides in him. — 1 John 4:16

God's love is the foundation upon which our love grows within us and moves us to love one another. The life of Saint Joseph provides us with a beautiful image of God's love as exemplified by Joseph's marriage to Mary and his acceptance of Jesus as his own beloved Son. The love between Mary, Joseph, and Jesus flowed from their strong faith in God.

Family can be our sanctuary, a refuge providing safety and security. But for our families to become our sanctuary, God must be at the center of our lives to lead and guide our actions. If we look at the lives of the Holy Family, Mary said "yes" to becoming the mother of Jesus, Joseph responded to God's command to care for Jesus and protect him, and Jesus' obedience to the will of the Father brought salvation to the world.

— Mary L. Kostic

In what ways does Saint Joseph inspire you to become a more holy family?

Prayer: Saint Joseph, teach us to bring the love of God to the center of our families and to freely share that love to all who enter into our lives. Amen.

Third Week of Lent, Friday

The Lord passed before him, and proclaimed, "The Lord, the Lord, a God merciful and gracious, slow to anger, and abounding in mercy and faithfulness, keeping merciful love for thousands" — Exodus 34:6–7

Love is the deepest desire and need of the human heart. There is affectionate love, romantic love, enduring love, familiar love, self-love, selfless love, sacrificial love. But the love of a father is singular, formative, protective. Fathers instill a sense of safety, well-being, security, and protection. They emulate God as our first protector. Joseph is all these things.

I try to imagine what went through the mind and heart of Joseph as his life unfolded with this call to be a husband to Mary and a father to her child. As a devout Jewish man, perhaps his heart recalled this verse from Exodus. It would have been impossible for Joseph to walk the journey with unfailing trust, faithfulness, and courage if he did not know that love is God's name. Joseph knew that his Father in heaven was with him, loving him and his family.

— Colleen Case

WHERE DO YOU NEED God's protection? God's provision? Where do you need the love of the Father in your life?

Prayer: Blessed Saint Joseph, help us grow to know and trust in God's protecting and providential love for us. Amen.

Third Week of Lent, Saturday

For God so loved the world that he gave his only-begotten Son, that whoever believes in him should not perish but have eternal life. — John 3:16

Did Jesus somehow grow to understand the Father in heaven by the actions of his father on earth? Saint Joseph is the visible human reflection of the Divine Love revealed in the Incarnation. In Saint Joseph, Jesus saw the tender love of God.

Growing up, Jesus worked beside Joseph in his carpentry shop, at home, and in the village where they lived. He witnessed mercy, love, and forgiveness Joseph offered others. These godly qualities formed Jesus and became visible when he began his public ministry. While Joseph did not live to see Jesus take up his mission, he was one of the first to believe that Christ was the Son of God given for the salvation of the world.

Saint Joseph demonstrated his unconditional love for the Holy Family on a daily basis as he protected them from all harm, raised Jesus as his own son, and acted as the faithful and chaste spouse of Mary.

— Sr. Mary McNulty

How have you experienced the love of God in your family? Friends? Coworkers?

Prayer: Saint Joseph, loving and beloved father of Jesus, who taught him love by example, show me the way to follow you. Amen.

~ Courage ~

Fourth Week of Lent, Sunday

I have said this to you, that in me you may have peace. In the world you have tribulation; but be of good cheer, I have overcome the world. — John 16:33

It is difficult to be courageous in a world of uncertainty. As the people of God, we know that we are pilgrims in this fleeting world; our true home is with God in heaven. This is why our hearts and minds should be centered on Jesus.

Although Joseph did not live to see the passion and Resurrection of his Son, he believed in the promises of God. He knew that God had been faithful to the people of Israel, and he believed and trusted in that faithfulness. This gave Joseph the courage to do what God asked of him.

Just the thought of being asked to live with the Son of God, let alone raise and protect him, must have felt daunting. Yet Joseph rose to the occasion. He took courage in the Lord because he knew Jesus was the fulfillment of God's promises, the Messiah who would conquer the world.

— Maria Pusateri

Do you have fears that are difficult to overcome? Today, take courage and focus your heart on the empty tomb.

Prayer: Saint Joseph, teach me to overcome my fears in the confidence that Jesus has conquered the world. Amen.

Fourth Week of Lent, Monday

"You are my servant,
I have chosen you and not cast you off";
fear not, for I am with you,
be not dismayed, for I am your God.
— Isaiah 41:9–10

Joseph displayed great courage when Jesus was lost for three days. Theologians have compared these three days that Jesus was lost in Joseph's life to what Mary suffered in the three days between the crucifixion and the Resurrection. In both situations, Jesus was gone and his parents, Joseph and Mary, experienced feelings of loss. Joseph had the confidence to walk into the unknown because he knew that God had chosen him, and was there with him.

The heart is where God rests within all of us, and it is where he transforms our doubts into trust, weaknesses into strength, and fear into courage. Let us turn to Saint Joseph to help us find the strength of God that lives within.

— Natalie Ryan

WHAT JOURNEY ARE YOU travelling right now? Have you lost Jesus? Ask Joseph to help you search for Christ.

Prayer: Saint Joseph, most courageous, help me today to embrace this beautiful and chaotic road. Guide me back to the center of my heart where God is at work. Amen.

Fourth Week of Lent, Tuesday

When I am afraid,
I put my trust in you.
In God, whose word I praise,
in God I trust without a fear.
— Psalm 56:3–4

As a faithful Jewish man, Joseph was familiar with this Scripture and probably prayed it frequently. This had an impact on his relationship with God. Joseph believed in God's faithfulness, and this awareness helped Joseph to be victorious over his fears and doubts. Joseph turned to the Lord for strength and courage, especially when he was afraid.

We live in a troubled world where many of us are anxious and fearful. But if we let fear and anxiety rule our lives, we will never be victorious over the sin of this world. Instead, we can follow in the footsteps of Joseph, who sought the Lord's help and strength in dealing with the adversities of life.

— Dr. Mary Amore

Reflect on the situations in your life that are causing fear and anxiety. How does the knowledge that God is trustworthy help you to overcome your feelings?

Prayer: Saint Joseph, you are a model of spiritual courage for me. Help me to follow your example, that I may faithfully turn to the Lord for strength to overcome the difficulties of life. Amen.

Fourth Week of Lent, Wednesday

Let not your heart faint, and be not fearful at the report heard in the land. — Jeremiah 51:46

Jeremiah was a prophet sent to the nation of Israel during the Babylonian exile to remind them of their need to put their trust in God, especially in national affairs. The times of Joseph and Mary were no different. Governments ruled apart from the needs of their people. Certain groups enjoyed privilege while others were being excluded. Sound familiar? How do we live as persons of faith in times of unsettling reports? Social injustices? News spreading like wildfire? Where do we anchor ourselves?

We do what Joseph did and find our strength in God. We take courage. We practice diligence. We look to God our source and summit, our provider, and our protector. Each day, we bring it all to him. This verse resonates with what we experience in the world today. There are always "rumors heard in the land."

— Colleen Case

WHERE HAVE YOU LOST courage lately? Where have you let the reports of the day steal your faith? Bring it all to your heavenly Father.

Prayer: Blessed Saint Joseph, help us to be people of courage. Help us to walk in the knowledge that God goes before us in all things and is with us in all things. Amen.

Fourth Week of Lent, Thursday

For you, O Lord of hosts, the God of Israel, have made this revelation to your servant, saying, "I will build you a house"; therefore your servant has found courage to pray this prayer to you. — 2 Samuel 7:27

When the solution to a challenging situation is easy, it does not take much effort to make a decision. When faced with a difficult problem, however, we must find strength within to make a courageous choice. Necessary decisions can sometimes be counterintuitive. But with prayerful discernment, we may see that God is directing us to address our particular circumstances.

Joseph's courage stemmed from his great love for God and for Mary. The challenge Joseph faced was that Jewish law dictated that an unfaithful and pregnant bride should be stoned to death. He would not allow this. After prayerful discernment, Joseph received a message from the angel and built his house around Mary in accordance with the God of Israel.

— Nanci Lukasik-Smith

How does courage play a part in your discernment and decision making?

Prayer: Saint Joseph, your amazing example of courage and strength gives me hope. Your prayers to heaven revealed that you were to build a home for the Holy Family. Come to my aid and help me to make a courageous choice that I may follow the will of God. Amen.

Fourth Week of Lent, Friday

Be watchful, stand firm in your faith, be courageous, be strong. — 1 Corinthians 16:13

Each day, I wake up to the ordinariness of life. Routine activities fill my days: preparing meals, caring for my family, work, and volunteering, with little thought of courage. Yet courage is part of our daily life. We do not have to go far from home to be courageous, for we never know what this day will bring. We are courageous in the daily choices we make that touch our hearts deeply and lead us to action for the greater good.

Joseph modeled courage when he took upon himself all the challenges he faced in the early events of his life with Mary. He was courageous in taking a pregnant bride on a long journey, then fleeing with his family to a foreign country, and eventually returning home to Nazareth. Joseph faced fear each time he responded to God speaking to him; but Joseph overcame his fears by faith. We can overcome our fears as Joseph did, by trusting more deeply in God.

— Joanne McElroy

WHAT FEARS ARE YOU facing where God is asking you to be courageous?

Prayer: Saint Joseph, help me to face my fears, to be courageous and trust in the Lord. Amen.

Fourth Week of Lent, Saturday

Joseph, son of David, do not fear to take Mary your wife, for that which is conceived in her is of the Holy Spirit. — *Matthew 1:20*

The root of the word courage is *cor*, or heart. Courage resides in the human heart and is nourished by lovingly caring for others. Saint Joseph was courageous in his own quiet way, responding to difficult situations out of the deep love he had for God and his beloved spouse, Mary. Throughout his entire life, Joseph found the courage to do the right thing, not because he was particularly fearless, but because his love was strong.

Courage often grows in and through hardship. The life of Saint Joseph shows us how to be brave in the face of adversity. Joseph's quiet courage, once embraced, remained with him.

— Dr. Jill Bates

Recall a time when courage was called for. How did you respond to the situation? Ask Saint Joseph for the gift of a loving heart, one in which courage is formed.

Prayer: Saint Joseph, thank you for showing me how to be a loving and courageous family member. Help me to remain faithful and loving in fulfilling what God has asked of me. Amen.

~ Self-Control ~

Fifth Week of Lent, Sunday

He who is slow to anger is better than the mighty,
and he who rules his spirit than he who takes a city.
— Proverbs 16:32

Whether it was in a gesture given to a driver who cut us off, or a sharp response spoken to a family member in exhaustion, or an entire cheesecake consumed, at one point or another we have all lost self-control.

In our world, the lack of self-control is almost glorified. "Have it your way" is the mantra of Hollywood, with pleasure and gratification featured on every commercial, movie, TV show, and magazine. We have almost lost all sense of the virtue of self-control.

Joseph, a humble and righteous man, practiced self-control over his spirit, mind, and body. He was able to resist temptation because he ruled his own spirit and was able to say "no" to himself.

— Cheri Hill, CPSD

What area of your mind, body, or spirit is aching for more self-control?

Prayer: Saint Joseph, model of self-control, I need your guidance with self-control in the area of __________________. Please intercede for me so that I may be able to surrender more fully to the will of God. Amen.

Fifth Week of Lent, Monday

No temptation has overtaken you that is not common to man. God is faithful, and he will not let you be tempted beyond your strength, but with the temptation will also provide the way of escape. — 1 Corinthians 10:13

Self-control can be manifested in many ways: staying calm when dealing with difficult friends or co-workers, not letting frustration with a spouse or child turn into anger and resentment, staying on schedule when we'd rather do something else. Losing self-control can be tempting because it offers an easy and immediate way out of a situation that often satisfies our preferences. It takes strength to have self-control, and faith that God never gives us more than we can handle.

As a man of profound faith, Joseph knew that the Lord would never give him more than he could handle. His trust in God allowed him to maintain self-control in both small, daily challenges and in situations that were more complex.

— Dr. Elizabeth McGovern

WHAT MAKES IT HARD for you to practice self-control?

Prayer: Saint Joseph, when I am struggling and want to give in and let temptation get the better of me, help me to remember that God has faith in me to do what is right and has given me the strength to do it. Amen.

Fifth Week of Lent, Tuesday

Know this, my beloved brethren. Let every man be quick to hear, slow to speak, slow to anger, for the anger of man does not work the righteousness of God. — James 1:19–20

God's plan for us is to live a moral life that includes prudence and self-control. Being quick to hear demonstrates the importance of active listening, listening that requires us to be patient and withhold judgements. By actively listening and thinking before we speak, we keep impatience and anger in check.

Saint Joseph is a role model for living prudently. When faced with a perplexing situation, such as Mary's unplanned pregnancy, Joseph prayerfully discerned his response before taking action. He exhibited self-control in his resistance to acting rashly before the angel appeared to him in a dream. Saint Joseph then put aside his feelings and accepted the word of the Lord in order to fulfill God's will. He was a patient and righteous man, who was quick to hear, slow to speak, and slow to anger.

— Donna Wierzgacz Soukup

What habits sustain you in developing self-control when impatient or angry?

Prayer: Saint Joseph, guide me to live prudently by developing self-control. Help me to listen. Assist me in avoiding being impatient and angry so that the righteousness of God may be worked in and through me. Amen.

Fifth Week of Lent, Wednesday

For the grace of God has appeared for the salvation of all men, training us to renounce irreligion and worldly passions. — Titus 2:11–12

Joseph did not rely on his own strength, for that would have failed him. Instead, he opened his heart to God's grace. Joseph's profound desire to do the will of God sustained him in the challenging circumstances he encountered as head of the Holy Family. Growing up, Jesus witnessed how his earthly father used this virtue to conquer the temptations of this world.

Each generation is tempted by "worldly passions" that can distract from godliness. With the help of the Holy Spirit, we can resist empty temptations and remain faithful to God as did Saint Joseph. Practicing self-control can lead to perseverance. Both are necessary qualities for living a godly life amid everyday challenges to our Christian faith and values. In his role as husband and father, Saint Joseph exemplified moderation, restraint, and the ability to say "no" to anything that fell short of God's calling.

— Bernadette Beyer, LMFT

What is the biggest obstacle I encounter to practicing self-control?

Prayer: Saint Joseph, I pray for your guidance in my relationship with God and with loved ones. May God's grace help me to persevere and remain committed to a godly life. Amen.

Fifth Week of Lent, Thursday

Know this, my beloved brethren. Let every man be quick to hear, slow to speak, slow to anger, for the anger of man does not work the righteousness of God. — James 1:19–20

When was the last time you lacked self-control? Was it anger at the car in front of you going slower than you thought it should, or the clerk at the grocery store taking longer than you thought necessary, or the crying toddler next to you in church? Our self-control is tested through many situations every day. Even the most patient person may find it difficult to perfectly master self-control.

It was evident in Joseph's everyday life that this humble, caring, and hardworking man of God had many reasons to react to the situations he had to face. But being the man that he was, having faith and trust in God, he realized that God was in control of his life. Joseph did all that the Lord asked him to do without challenge, with self-control, and in silence.

— Mary L. Kostic

Our heavenly Father expects us to nurture his gift of self-control by reading God's word, meditating on his word, and imitating Joseph's self-control in our everyday lives.

Prayer: Saint Joseph, Guardian of Jesus, humble servant of Our Lord, help me to bear my cross with self-control. Amen.

Fifth Week of Lent, Friday

But the Counselor, the Holy Spirit, whom the Father will send in my name, he will teach you all things, and bring to your remembrance all that I have said to you. —*John 14:26*

The Holy Spirit teaches and reminds us that displaying temperance in moments of emotional or stressful situations reveals the fruit of self-control. The ability to make choices about how we feel, act, and respond to others demonstrates an active participation in the divine gifts we have received, and offers us the opportunity to draw closer to God and others.

Joseph relied on the Spirit of God to work with him to overcome the immense challenges he faced. The Holy Spirit was an active part of Joseph's life. The divine presence continually advocated on behalf of the Holy Family. By avoiding extreme behavior and exercising restraint, Joseph demonstrated the gift of self-control in lovingly leading and guiding Mary and Jesus through the joys and challenges of family life.

— Naomi Lukasik-Smith

THINK ABOUT THE LAST time you lost control of yourself in a situation. How can you rely on the fruit of self-control to guide you the next time a challenge arises?

Prayer: Saint Joseph, in times of pressure or temptation, you remained in control. Help me to release the need to be impulsive and prevent me from being overwhelmed in a moment of disagreement. Amen.

Fifth Week of Lent, Saturday

For this very reason make every effort to supplement your faith with virtue, and virtue with knowledge, and knowledge with self-control, and self-control with steadfastness, and steadfastness with godliness, and godliness with brotherly affection, and brotherly affection with love. — 2 Peter 1:5–7

If practicing the virtue of self-control in one situation is difficult, the ability to maintain self-control throughout the course of a lifetime seems impossible. Yet this is what Joseph was able to accomplish. Joseph controlled his emotions in even the most difficult of times, because he trusted the Lord was guiding him.

I remember when our children were newborns. They were so tiny and frail that I knew I would do anything to keep them safe. I cannot imagine what Joseph experienced at the birth of Jesus. How did he feel when he could not provide a safe environment for Mary to give birth? Or when groups of smelly shepherds with animals sought out his newborn Son? Saint Joseph's life reminds us that the way to maintain self-control is to place complete faith and trust in God.

— Dr. Mary Amore

In which areas of your life do you find it easy to practice self-control?

Prayer: Saint Joseph, help me to maintain self-control over matters big and small, that I may grow in my faith. Amen.

~ Holy Week ~

Palm Sunday

Hosanna! Blessed is he who comes in the name of the Lord! Blessed is the kingdom of our father David that is coming! Hosanna in the highest!
— Mark 11:9–10

As palm branches are spread before him, Jesus is hailed by those in the crowds as King of Israel, a title very different from that of his childhood when he was known as "the carpenter's son."

Growing up, my dad was an advocate for higher education, especially for women. Unfortunately, he never lived to see me begin my graduate studies. Nevertheless, when I received my Doctor of Ministry degree, I felt my father's presence with me.

I think it possible Jesus felt Joseph's presence as he rode triumphantly into Jerusalem. Perhaps Joseph's fatherly presence comforted Jesus as he embarked on the journey toward his destiny. This Palm Sunday, let us join our prayers to Joseph's as together we proclaim, *Blessed is he who comes in the name of the Lord! Hosanna in the highest!*

— Dr. Mary Amore

Have people ever questioned your ability to do something just because of your family background? Seek the help of Saint Joseph to assist you in becoming who God created you to be.

Prayer: Saint Joseph, be with me this week as I journey with Jesus from death to new life. Amen.

Monday

Behold my servant, whom I uphold,
my chosen, in whom my soul delights;
I have put my Spirit upon him,
he will bring forth justice to the nations.
He will not cry or lift up his voice,
or make it heard in the street.
— Isaiah 42:1–2

The prophet Isaiah speaks of the coming of Jesus. In a beautiful way, he also depicts the person of Joseph, a servant of the Lord. In the Gospels, Joseph's voice is silent, he utters no words, he does not cry out, and he does not make his voice heard in the street. Rather, we know Joseph by his actions, which showed him to be a man of peace and justice, bravely caring for his family with the unwavering love of a father and spouse.

I have lived almost half of my life without my parents; yet their presence is with me every day. No one knows how old Jesus was at the time that Joseph left this earth; but Jesus surely carried Joseph's love with him from the crèche to the cross.

— Dr. Mary Amore

Reflect on the bonds of love that you share with your family members, both living and deceased. Thank the Lord for their presence.

Prayer: Saint Joseph, help me to be a gentle and kind person, offering love to all those who God sends my way. Amen.

Tuesday

The Lord is my light and my salvation; whom shall I fear?
I believe that I shall see the goodness of the Lord
in the land of the living!
Wait for the Lord;
be strong, and let your heart take courage;
yes, wait for the Lord!
— *Psalm 27:1,13–14*

Joseph spent his entire life believing that he would see the bounty of the Lord. He was a faithful Jew who was well-versed in Sacred Scripture and most assuredly prayed this particular psalm, especially when he was fearful. His faith remained steadfast, and the Lord was his light and salvation.

Joseph was not there to see Jesus betrayed at the hands of those who knew him, nor could he protect his Son from what was to come. In those dark days leading to the crucifixion, surely Jesus thought of Joseph and wished his earthly father were there to comfort him and his mother, Mary, as he had done for them in the past.

— Dr. Mary Amore

What people or events are causing you to worry? Seek the assistance of Saint Joseph to help you find courage.

Prayer: Saint Joseph, you protected the Holy Family. Watch over me and help me to overcome my fears, that I may wait for the Lord with courage. Amen.

Wednesday

Then one of the Twelve, who was called Judas Iscariot, went to the chief priests and said, "What will you give me if I deliver him to you?" And they paid him thirty pieces of silver. And from that moment he sought an opportunity to betray him. — Matthew 26:14

The Wednesday of Holy Week is historically known as "Spy Wednesday," because it marks the day when Judas Iscariot betrayed Jesus. It is difficult for us to imagine how Judas could boldly betray his friend, Jesus, for money, but he did.

Growing up, Jesus surely watched Joseph sell and barter his carpentry goods and services in exchange for valuable commodities such as salt, or precious metals like bronze, silver, and gold. While Joseph was able to shield Jesus from the actions of murderous kings, he could not have imagined that someday Jesus would be sold for thirty pieces of silver at the hands of a trusted friend.

The legacy of Saint Joseph shows us that no matter how difficult a situation may be, we are to remain faithful to the Lord.

— Dr. Mary Amore

Have you ever betrayed someone? How did this make you feel? Have you attempted to heal this relationship?

Prayer: Saint Joseph, you are a man of utmost integrity. Help me to treat others as I would like to be treated. Amen.

Holy Thursday

If I then, your Lord and Teacher, have washed your feet, you also ought to wash one another's feet. For I have given you an example, that you also should do as I have done to you. — John 13:14–15

In the time of Jesus, people either walked barefoot or wore sandals. Washing one's feet was a daily ritual, and one that Joseph surely did for Jesus as he was growing up. I can imagine Joseph keeling down on the floor, looking up at his Son with love. Day after day, Jesus experienced this humble ritual of love offered by his father and this experience stayed with Jesus as he grew up and began his public ministry.

Foot washing always reminds me of my mom. Shortly before she died, she accidently spilled something on her socks, so I had to wash off her feet. As I knelt down and held her tiny feet in my hands, I was overcome with emotion as I realized what a privilege it was for me to wash the feet of my mother, the woman who had cared for me.

— Dr. Mary Amore

Consider your own life. How can you serve the needs of others with love and humility?

Prayer: Saint Joseph, help me to lovingly serve all those the Lord sends my way. Amen.

Good Friday

Surely he has borne our griefs
and carried our sorrows;
yet we esteemed him stricken,
struck down by God, and afflicted.
But he was wounded for our transgressions …
upon him was the chastisement that made us whole,
and with his stripes we are healed.
— Isaiah 53:4–5

It is likely that Joseph spent years preparing Jesus for his mission, yet we do not know if Joseph fully understood the extent of that mission, or that his son, Jesus, would fulfill this prophecy.

Years ago, my sister-in-law died of bone cancer. As she struggled in the final stages of her painful disease, I remember watching my mother-in-law agonize over her daughter's illness. She kept telling me it should have been her, and not Joanne. She felt helpless that she could not protect her daughter from suffering and death. The same can be said of Jesus and Joseph. The love they shared as father and son went with Jesus as he journeyed to the cross, and accompanied him as he died.

— Dr. Mary Amore

Saint Joseph is the Patron Saint of a Happy Death. Ask Saint Joseph to pray that you and your loved ones may experience a peaceful death.

Prayer: Saint Joseph, beloved foster father of Jesus, take me by the hand and lead me safely to your Son, Jesus. Amen.

Holy Saturday

I said, In the noontide of my days
I must depart;
I am consigned to the gates of Sheol
for the rest of my years.
— Isaiah 38:10

An ancient first century homily proclaims that Jesus "raised up all those who ever slept since the world began … he has gone in search of Adam, our first father, as for a lost sheep, greatly desiring to visit those who live in darkness and in the shadow of death." Surely, in the shadows between the crucifixion and the Resurrection, Jesus searched for Joseph. What a glorious reunion this must have been. An ancient homily beautifully describes what might have transpired between the two as they were reunited on Holy Saturday: "The cherubim throne has been prepared, the bearers are ready and waiting, the food is provided, the everlasting houses and rooms are in readiness; the treasures of good things have been opened; the kingdom of heaven has been prepared before the ages." Come, Father, be with me forever this day in paradise.

— Dr. Mary Amore

Invite Saint Joseph to help prepare your heart and soul to be ready to meet the Lord when he comes.

Prayer: Saint Joseph, help me to follow your example of faith, that I may one day be united with you and Jesus in the glorious kingdom of heaven. Amen.

Easter Sunday

And entering the tomb, they saw a young man sitting on the right side, dressed in a white robe; and they were amazed. And he said to them, "Do not be amazed; you seek Jesus of Nazareth, who was crucified. He has risen, he is not here." — Mark 16:5–6

When Mary received news of Christ's resurrection, her heart must have filled with unspeakable joy. At that moment, Mary likely thought of her beloved husband, Joseph, and wished to share this incredible joy with him.

Shortly after my parents died, I heard some exciting news about one of our relatives and I instinctively reached for the phone to call my parents. Our loved ones live in our hearts and in our memories. The Holy Family was no different. Mary and Joseph loved Jesus, and the miraculous news of him rising from the dead would certainly have brought joy, hope, and peace to the Holy Family, here and in heaven.

Let us ask Saint Joseph, earthly father of Jesus, to help us live as Easter people each day, for Jesus is risen from the dead and all creation sings, "Alleluia!"

— Dr. Mary Amore

How does the glory of the Resurrection bring hope to your life?

Prayer: Saint Joseph, help me love Jesus as you loved him, and to live each day in loving service to him. Amen.

Dr. Mary Amore holds a Doctor of Ministry Degree in Liturgical Studies and a Master of Arts in Pastoral Studies from Catholic Theological Union. A published author and national presenter, Dr. Amore is the editor and cocontributor of *Every Day with Mary*. Married, the mother of two adult children and grandmother of two grandchildren, Dr. Amore currently serves as the full-time executive director of Mayslake Ministries.

ALSO AVAILABLE

Every Day with Saint Joseph

Mary Amore, Editor

Every Day with Saint Joseph is the perfect place to start building that relationship. With a timely and relevant meditation for each day of the year, this book will help you connect with Joseph even in the midst of your busy life. This daily devotional is divided into twelve months, with each month highlighting a particular spiritual gift or charism that Saint Joseph exhibited as the husband of Mary and the foster father of Jesus. You'll begin each day with a quotation from Scripture, followed by a brief reflection, a question or act to consider, and a short prayer to Saint Joseph to carry through your day.

Available at
OSVCatholicBookstore.com
or wherever books are sold